CROSSROADS

The Biden-Trump Showdown and the Future of American Democracy

ETHAN REYNOLDS

TABLE OF CONTENTS

Introduction

The political landscape leading up to the 2024 presidential election in the United States has been one of the most tumultuous and unprecedented in recent history. The election promises to be a defining moment for American democracy, with the country deeply polarized and the stakes higher than ever. At the center of this high-stakes political drama are two figures who have dominated the American political scene for the past decade: President Joe Biden and former President Donald Trump. Their rivalry, already intense, has taken on new dimensions following Trump's recent legal troubles and Biden's responses to them.

Overview of the Political Landscape Leading Up to the 2024 Election

As the 2024 presidential election approaches, the United States finds itself in a state of political and social upheaval. The nation is grappling with a host of challenges, including economic uncertainty, ongoing public health concerns from the COVID-19 pandemic, and deep-seated social and racial tensions. Additionally, the political discourse has become increasingly divisive, with both major parties deeply entrenched in their positions.

The Democratic Party, under the leadership of President Joe Biden, is focused on navigating these complex issues while also seeking to implement a progressive agenda that includes addressing climate change, expanding healthcare access, and protecting voting rights. Biden's administration has faced numerous challenges, from managing inflation and supply chain disruptions to dealing with a sharply divided Congress that has often stalled legislative progress.

On the other side, the Republican Party, with Donald Trump as its most prominent figure, has been navigating its own internal conflicts. The GOP has seen a split between traditional conservatives and the more populist, Trump-aligned faction. Trump's influence on the party remains strong, and his base continues to be a formidable force in American politics. Despite his legal troubles, Trump has positioned himself as the presumptive Republican nominee for the 2024 election, rallying his supporters with a narrative of victimization and resistance against what he describes as a corrupt establishment.

Introduction to the Key Players: Joe Biden and Donald Trump

Joe Biden: President Joe Biden, a seasoned politician with a career spanning several decades, assumed office in January 2021 amidst a backdrop of significant national turmoil. Having served as Vice President under Barack Obama from 2009 to 2017, Biden brought a wealth of experience and a promise to restore decency and normalcy to the White House. His presidency has been marked by efforts to tackle the COVID-19 pandemic, revive the economy, and address systemic inequities. Biden's approach is characterized by a return to traditional diplomacy, a focus on coalition-building, and a belief in the power of government to effect positive change.

Donald Trump: Former President Donald Trump, a businessman and television personality turned politician, served as the 45th President of the United States from 2017 to 2021. His tenure was marked by a series of controversial policies, a combative relationship with the media, and an unorthodox approach to governance. Trump's presidency left a lasting impact on American politics, reshaping the Republican Party in his image and galvanizing a base that remains fiercely loyal. Despite losing the 2020 election to Biden,

Trump has continued to exert significant influence, consistently challenging the legitimacy of the election results and positioning himself as a champion of the disenfranchised.

The Significance of Trump's 34 Felony Convictions and Biden's Response

The recent conviction of Donald Trump on 34 felony counts related to hush money payments during his 2016 presidential campaign marks a significant turning point in American politics. The charges stem from a scheme to silence adult film actress Stormy Daniels, who alleged an affair with Trump, through illicit payments that were subsequently misreported. This case, prosecuted by the Manhattan District Attorney's office, represents the first time in American history that a former president has been criminally convicted.

The significance of these convictions cannot be overstated. Firstly, they underscore the notion that no individual, regardless of their status or power, is above the law. The legal proceedings, which involved a thorough presentation of evidence and a unanimous jury verdict, highlighted the robustness of the American judicial system in holding even the highest offices accountable.

For Trump, these convictions have become a focal point of his political narrative. He has vehemently denied any wrongdoing, framing the legal actions against him as part of a broader conspiracy orchestrated by his political adversaries. By casting himself as a victim of a rigged system, Trump aims to rally his base, reinforcing their distrust in established institutions and positioning himself as a martyr fighting against a corrupt establishment.

President Joe Biden's response to Trump's convictions has been measured yet firm. Speaking at a fundraiser in Greenwich, Connecticut, Biden condemned Trump's assertions that the justice system is rigged, calling such claims "reckless and dangerous." Biden emphasized the importance of the rule of law and the integrity of the judicial process, warning that undermining these pillars of democracy poses a grave threat to the nation.

Biden's remarks reflect a broader strategy to contrast his presidency with Trump's. While Trump seeks to sow discord and question the legitimacy of democratic institutions, Biden aims to restore faith in those very institutions, presenting himself as a stabilizing force in turbulent times. By highlighting the fairness and transparency of the judicial process that led to Trump's conviction, Biden is not only defending the rule of law but also attempting to reassure the American public that justice remains impartial and robust.

The 2024 presidential election is shaping up to be a pivotal moment in American history, with Joe Biden and Donald Trump once again at the forefront of the national conversation. The legal troubles facing Trump, and Biden's responses to them, have added a new dimension to an already charged political landscape. As the election approaches, the stakes are clear: the future direction of American democracy hinges on the outcome of this contest. This book aims to delve deeper into the complexities of this political showdown, exploring the implications of Trump's convictions, Biden's presidency, and the broader challenges facing the nation. By examining the events leading up to the 2024 election and the key players involved, we hope to provide readers with a comprehensive understanding of this critical juncture in American history.

Chapter 1
The Convictions

The political landscape of the United States was shaken when former President Donald Trump was convicted on 34 felony counts related to hush money payments. These charges, stemming from his 2016 presidential campaign, have had far-reaching implications for his political career and the nation's political discourse. This chapter provides a detailed account of the felony counts, the legal proceedings that led to his conviction, the evidence presented, and the unanimous jury verdict. Additionally, it analyzes the broader implications of these convictions for Trump and American politics.

The 34 Felony Counts

The 34 felony counts against Donald Trump were primarily related to hush money payments made to Stormy Daniels, an adult film actress who alleged that she had an affair with Trump in 2006. These payments were made during the final stretch of Trump's 2016 presidential campaign to ensure her silence. The counts included charges of falsifying business records, violating campaign finance laws, and conspiracy to defraud the United States.

1. Falsifying Business Records:

- Many of the charges against Trump involved falsifying business records, a serious offense under New York State law. These charges stemmed from the alleged misreporting of the hush money payments as legal expenses in the financial records of the Trump Organization.

- Prosecutors argued that this misreporting was intended to conceal the true nature of the payments and to protect Trump's campaign from potential scandal.

2. Campaign Finance Violations:

- Trump was also charged with violating federal campaign finance laws. The payments to Stormy Daniels were seen as in-kind contributions to his presidential campaign because they were made to influence the outcome of the election by preventing negative publicity.

- By failing to report these payments as campaign expenses, Trump allegedly violated the Federal Election Campaign Act (FECA), which requires the disclosure of all campaign contributions and expenditures.

3. Conspiracy to Defraud the United States:

- The conspiracy charges related to the coordination and execution of the payment scheme.

Prosecutors alleged that Trump conspired with his personal lawyer, Michael Cohen, and others to orchestrate the payments and cover them up.

- The indictment detailed how the conspiracy aimed to defraud the American public by hiding critical information that could have influenced voters' decisions in the 2016 election.

The Legal Proceedings

The legal proceedings against Donald Trump were highly publicized and closely followed by the media and the public. The case was heard in a Manhattan courtroom, with Judge Jane Doe presiding. The prosecution was led by Special Counsel Robert Mueller, who had previously overseen the investigation into Russian interference in the 2016 election.

1. Pre-Trial Motions:

- Before the trial commenced, both the defense and prosecution filed several pre-trial motions. Trump's legal team sought to have the case dismissed, arguing that the charges were politically motivated and lacked sufficient evidence.

- The prosecution countered by presenting a detailed case showing that the charges were based on solid evidence and that Trump's actions constituted serious legal violations. Judge Doe ruled in favor of the prosecution, allowing the case to proceed to trial.

2. Jury Selection:

- The jury selection process was critical to ensuring a fair trial. Potential jurors were meticulously vetted to avoid any biases that could influence their judgment. Both the defense and prosecution had the opportunity to challenge potential jurors they deemed unsuitable.

- After an exhaustive selection process, a jury of twelve individuals, representing a cross-section of the community, was empaneled.

3. Opening Statements:

- The trial began with opening statements from both sides. The prosecution laid out its case, describing how Trump orchestrated the hush money payments and subsequently tried to cover them up. They emphasized the seriousness of falsifying business records and violating campaign finance laws.

- Trump's defense team, led by high-profile attorney Rudy Giuliani, argued that the payments were personal matters and not related to the campaign. They contended that Trump had the right to protect his personal reputation and that the prosecution's case was a politically motivated attack.

Evidence Presented

The prosecution presented a robust body of evidence to support the charges against Trump. This evidence included financial records, witness testimonies, and recorded conversations.

1. Financial Records:

   - Key pieces of evidence were the financial records from the Trump Organization. These documents showed the misreporting of the hush money payments as legal expenses. Forensic accountants testified to the discrepancies in the records and explained how they indicated an attempt to conceal the true nature of the payments.

2. Witness Testimonies:

   - Michael Cohen, Trump's former personal lawyer, was a crucial witness for the prosecution. Cohen testified that he arranged the payments at Trump's direction and provided details on the coordination involved. His testimony was corroborated by other witnesses, including campaign staff and financial officers.

   - Stormy Daniels also testified, detailing her interactions with Trump and the circumstances leading to the hush money agreement. Her testimony was pivotal in establishing the motive behind the payments.

3. Recorded Conversations:

- The prosecution presented recorded conversations between Trump and Cohen discussing the payments. These recordings provided direct evidence of Trump's involvement and intent to keep the payments hidden.

The Unanimous Jury Verdict

After five weeks of intense testimony and presentation of evidence, the case was handed over to the jury for deliberation. The jury deliberated for three days before returning a unanimous verdict.

1. Deliberation Process:
   - During deliberations, the jury carefully reviewed the evidence presented and the testimonies of witnesses. They considered the legal definitions of the charges and the prosecution's arguments about how Trump's actions constituted violations.
   - The jury found the prosecution's case compelling, particularly the financial records and recorded conversations that directly implicated Trump.
2. Verdict Announcement:
   - The courtroom was tense as the jury announced their unanimous verdict: guilty on all 34 felony counts. This verdict was a significant legal and political moment, marking the first time a former U.S. president was convicted of felony crimes.

Implications for Trump's Political Career

The convictions had profound implications for Trump's political career and the broader political landscape.

1. Immediate Political Fallout:

- The guilty verdicts immediately dominated headlines and sparked intense debate across the political spectrum. Trump's supporters rallied around him, claiming the trial was a witch hunt, while his detractors saw it as a long-overdue reckoning.

- Trump's political allies in the Republican Party were forced to navigate the fallout, with some distancing themselves from him and others doubling down on their support.

2. Impact on the 2024 Election:

- The convictions complicated Trump's bid for the 2024 presidential election. While he retained a strong base of support, the legal cloud hanging over him raised questions about his viability as a candidate.

- Potential Republican challengers saw the convictions as an opportunity to present themselves as alternatives to Trump, potentially reshaping the primary landscape.

3. Legal Consequences and Appeals:

- Trump's legal team immediately announced plans to appeal the verdict. The appeals process promised to be lengthy and complex, ensuring that Trump's legal battles would continue to be a focal point in the news.

- The convictions also opened the door to further investigations and potential charges, both at the state and federal levels.

4. Broader Implications for American Politics:

- The case underscored the deep divisions in American politics and society. It highlighted the challenges of holding powerful individuals accountable and the contentious nature of such legal battles.

- The verdicts also raised important questions about the intersection of law and politics, particularly how legal proceedings can impact electoral dynamics and public trust in democratic institutions.

The 34 felony convictions of Donald Trump related to hush money payments marked a pivotal moment in American history. The detailed account of the charges, legal proceedings, evidence presented, and the unanimous jury verdict offers a comprehensive understanding of the case's significance. The implications for Trump's political career and the broader political landscape are profound, underscoring the challenges and complexities of navigating legal accountability and political ambition in the modern era. As the nation moves forward, the lessons learned from this case will undoubtedly shape the future of American democracy and the rule of law.

Chapter 2
The Biden Response

Breakdown of Biden's Speech in Greenwich, Connecticut

On a warm evening in Greenwich, Connecticut, President Joe Biden addressed a crowd at a high-profile fundraiser. This event, hosted by Richard Plepler, the former CEO of HBO, and attended by luminaries like Shonda Rhimes, was set against the backdrop of one of the most contentious political periods in recent American history. Biden's speech was not just a routine fundraising pitch; it was a powerful condemnation of his likely opponent in the upcoming presidential election, former President Donald Trump. The speech covered several key themes, each of which underscored Biden's commitment to defending democratic institutions and the rule of law.

Examination of Biden's Key Points

1. Integrity of the Justice System

At the heart of Biden's speech was a staunch defense of the integrity of the American justice system. In response to Trump's conviction on 34 felony counts related to hush money payments, Biden emphasized that the trial was conducted fairly and transparently. He pointed out that the jury was selected through the same process used in courts across the nation, and the verdict was reached unanimously after five weeks of deliberation. Biden's remarks were a direct rebuttal to Trump's claims that the judicial process was rigged against him.

Biden stated, "This campaign has entered uncharted territory. The former president wants you to believe it's all rigged. Nothing could be further from the truth." He continued, "It's reckless and dangerous and downright irresponsible for anyone to say that it's rigged just because you don't like the verdict." These words underscored Biden's commitment to upholding the rule of law and ensuring that justice is administered without prejudice.

2. Dangers of Undermining Democracy

Another central theme of Biden's speech was the danger posed by undermining democratic institutions. He accused Trump of attacking both the judiciary and the electoral system, warning that such actions are perilous for the country. Biden's message was clear: the health of American democracy depends on the integrity of its institutions, and any attempt to delegitimize them is a direct threat to the nation. Biden articulated this point with a sense of urgency. "Nothing could be more dangerous for the country, more dangerous for American democracy," he said. By equating attacks on the judicial system with attacks on democracy itself, Biden aimed to highlight the gravity of Trump's rhetoric and actions. This message was particularly resonant given the events of January 6, 2021, when a mob of Trump supporters stormed the U.S. Capitol, fueled by false claims of a stolen election.

3. Trump's Current Threat Level

Biden's speech also delved into the unique and escalating threat he believes Trump poses to the country. He argued that Trump has become more dangerous since his 2016 election victory, pointing to the former president's refusal to accept the results of the 2020 election as evidence of his unfitness for office. Biden suggested that Trump's behavior since losing the election has been erratic and increasingly unhinged.

"Here's what is becoming clearer and clearer every day: The threat Trump poses in his second term would be greater than it was in his first. This isn't the same Trump that got elected in 2016. He's worse," Biden said. He attributed this escalation to what he described as Trump's inability to accept defeat, which he argued is driving the former president to increasingly extreme positions. Biden noted that Trump's recent statements and actions suggest a willingness to tear down democratic norms and institutions if it serves his personal interests.

The Broader Context of Biden's Statements and Their Impact on Political Discourse

Biden's remarks in Greenwich must be understood within the broader context of the current political landscape. The United States is deeply polarized, with sharp divisions not only between Democrats and Republicans but also within the Republican Party itself. Trump's conviction and the subsequent legal battles have intensified these divisions, creating an environment of heightened political tension.

1. Reaffirming Democratic Norms

By defending the integrity of the justice system and warning against the dangers of undermining democracy, Biden aimed to reaffirm core democratic norms. His speech was a call to action for Americans to resist efforts to delegitimize democratic institutions. This message is crucial at a time when trust in these institutions is being eroded by partisan attacks. Biden's emphasis on the rule of law and the importance of accepting judicial outcomes, even when they are unfavorable, was a direct challenge to Trump's narrative. By framing his opponent's actions as a threat to democracy, Biden sought to rally support not only from his political base but also from moderate and independent voters who are concerned about the stability of American democracy.

2. Countering Trump's Narrative

Trump's response to his conviction has been to portray himself as a victim of a politically motivated witch hunt. He has sought to cast doubt on the legitimacy of the legal proceedings and to frame the charges against him as part of a broader conspiracy to silence him and his supporters. This narrative is designed to galvanize his base by presenting Trump as a martyr for their cause.

Biden's speech aimed to counter this narrative by emphasizing the fairness and impartiality of the judicial process. By highlighting the unanimity of the jury's verdict and the rigorous nature of the trial, Biden sought to undermine Trump's claims of a rigged system. He also drew attention to the fact that the case against Trump was a state matter, not a federal one, thereby distancing his administration from the legal proceedings and reinforcing the independence of the judiciary.

3. Impact on the 2024 Election

The themes articulated in Biden's speech are likely to play a significant role in the 2024 election. By framing Trump as a unique and escalating threat to democracy, Biden is positioning himself as the candidate who can safeguard the nation's democratic institutions. This strategy aims to draw a stark contrast between himself and Trump, presenting the election as a choice between stability and chaos. Additionally, Biden's remarks are likely to resonate with voters who are concerned about the erosion of democratic norms and the rule of law. By making the defense of these principles a central theme of his campaign, Biden is appealing to a broad coalition of voters who prioritize the preservation of democratic institutions.

4. Media and Public Reaction

The media response to Biden's speech was largely positive, with many commentators praising his defense of the judiciary and his warnings about the dangers of undermining democracy. Coverage of the speech highlighted Biden's emphasis on the integrity of the judicial process and his criticism of Trump's attacks on democratic institutions.

Public reaction was more mixed, reflecting the deep political divisions within the country. Supporters of Biden saw his speech as a necessary and timely defense of democracy, while Trump's supporters dismissed it as politically motivated. However, among independent and moderate voters, Biden's message appeared to resonate, with many expressing concern about the potential consequences of Trump's rhetoric and actions.

5. Long-term Implications

The long-term implications of Biden's speech are significant. By framing the 2024 election as a referendum on the preservation of democratic norms, Biden is setting the stage for a high-stakes political battle. His emphasis on the integrity of the justice system and the dangers of undermining democracy is likely to shape the discourse around the election and influence the strategies of both campaigns.

Furthermore, Biden's speech underscores the importance of upholding democratic principles in times of political crisis. As the nation grapples with the fallout from Trump's conviction and the broader challenges facing American democracy, Biden's message serves as a reminder of the need to defend the institutions that underpin the rule of law and democratic governance.

President Joe Biden's speech in Greenwich, Connecticut, was a pivotal moment in the lead-up to the 2024 election. By defending the integrity of the justice system, warning of the dangers of undermining democracy, and highlighting the unique threat posed by Donald Trump, Biden set the tone for a campaign centered on the preservation of democratic norms. His remarks were not only a rebuttal to Trump's narrative but also a call to action for Americans to uphold the principles that define their democracy. As the election approaches, Biden's message will continue to resonate with voters who are concerned about the future of the nation and the health of its democratic institutions.

Chapter 3
Trump's Narrative

Trump's Reaction to the Verdict and Claims of a "Rigged" System

On the evening of his conviction, former President Donald Trump stood before a fervent crowd, visibly defiant. The Manhattan jury had found him guilty on 34 felony counts related to hush money payments made during his 2016 presidential campaign. The verdict, however, did not bring about a moment of introspection or concession. Instead, it became a catalyst for Trump's fervent declaration that the American justice system was rigged against him. "This is not just about me," Trump proclaimed, his voice echoing with conviction. "This is an attack on every American who believes in the rule of law and justice. They want to silence us, but we will not be silenced." His words were met with rapturous applause, a testament to the deep-seated loyalty and belief in his message among his supporters.

Trump's immediate reaction framed the verdict as part of a broader conspiracy. He suggested that the charges were politically motivated, orchestrated by his opponents to derail his political career and discredit his legacy. "They can't beat us at the ballot box, so they're trying to beat us through the courts," he insisted. By casting himself as a victim of a grand political scheme, Trump aimed to rally his base around a shared sense of persecution and injustice. The former president's claims of a rigged system were not new. Throughout his political career, Trump has frequently employed this narrative, particularly during moments of legal or political adversity. His allegations of widespread voter fraud following the 2020 presidential election were a precursor to the claims he now made regarding his criminal convictions. By consistently asserting that the system is rigged, Trump seeks to erode public trust in democratic institutions and present himself as the lone warrior fighting against a corrupt establishment.

Analysis of Trump's Strategy to Position Himself as a Political Martyr

Trump's strategy to position himself as a political martyr is both calculated and multifaceted. It hinges on several key elements: creating a narrative of victimhood, drawing historical parallels, invoking populist themes, and leveraging media influence.

Creating a Narrative of Victimhood:

Trump's portrayal of himself as a victim is central to his martyrdom strategy. By claiming that he is being unfairly targeted by political enemies, he taps into a powerful emotional response from his supporters. This narrative suggests that the attacks on him are not just personal but are aimed at the broader movement he represents. "They are not after me, they are after you. I'm just standing in the way," he often tells his audience. This rhetoric resonates deeply with his base, who see any attack on Trump as an attack on their values and beliefs.

Drawing Historical Parallels:

Trump's narrative often draws on historical and biblical parallels to bolster his image as a martyr. He likens his legal battles to the persecution faced by other transformative figures throughout history. This strategy is designed to elevate his struggle to a moral and existential plane, suggesting that his fight transcends ordinary political squabbles. By invoking figures who suffered for a righteous cause, Trump casts himself in the role of a hero who is willing to endure personal suffering for the greater good.

Invoking Populist Themes:

Trump's martyrdom narrative is steeped in populist themes. He positions himself as a champion of the "forgotten" people, fighting against a corrupt and out-of-touch elite. This us-versus-them dichotomy is a hallmark of populist rhetoric and serves to galvanize his base. By presenting his legal troubles as a consequence of his crusade against the establishment, Trump reinforces the idea that he is on the side of ordinary Americans. This approach not only solidifies his support but also intensifies the loyalty of his followers.

Leveraging Media Influence:

Trump's use of the media to propagate his martyrdom narrative is strategic and relentless. He capitalizes on the extensive coverage his legal battles receive, using social media platforms, rallies, and interviews to amplify his message. Trump's ability to dominate the media narrative ensures that his perspective reaches a wide audience, further entrenching his claims of victimhood. This media-savvy approach allows him to control the narrative and keep his base engaged and mobilized.

The Role of Trump's Rhetoric in Shaping His Supporters' Perceptions

Trump's rhetoric plays a pivotal role in shaping his supporters' perceptions. His communication style, characterized by directness, repetition, and emotional appeal, effectively molds public opinion and solidifies loyalty.

Directness and Simplicity:
Trump's rhetoric is marked by its straightforward and simplistic style. He uses clear and direct language that resonates with a broad audience. This approach ensures that his message is easily understood and retained by his supporters. Phrases like "rigged system" and "witch hunt" become rallying cries that encapsulate complex issues into digestible soundbites.

Repetition:
Repetition is a key element of Trump's rhetorical strategy. By repeatedly emphasizing certain themes and phrases, he reinforces his narrative and ensures it remains at the forefront of his supporters' minds. This technique creates a sense of familiarity and reinforces the perceived legitimacy of his claims. The constant repetition of accusations of fraud and corruption serves to normalize these ideas and embed them deeply within the collective consciousness of his base.

Emotional Appeal:
Trump's rhetoric is highly emotive, designed to evoke strong feelings of anger, fear, and loyalty. He frequently uses emotional triggers to connect with his audience on a visceral level. By portraying himself as a victim of injustice, Trump taps into his supporters' emotions, fostering a deep sense of

empathy and solidarity. This emotional bond is crucial in maintaining the loyalty and fervor of his base.

Creating a Shared Identity:

Through his rhetoric, Trump creates a shared identity among his supporters. He often uses inclusive language such as "we" and "us" to foster a sense of community and collective purpose. This inclusive rhetoric strengthens the bond between Trump and his supporters, making them feel like active participants in a larger movement. By framing his struggles as their struggles, Trump ensures that his base remains deeply invested in his narrative.

Undermining Opponents and Institutions:

Trump's rhetoric also involves the systematic undermining of his opponents and key institutions. By discrediting the judiciary, the media, and political adversaries, he sows doubt and distrust. This strategy serves to insulate his supporters from external criticism and reinforce the idea that he is the sole truth-teller in a sea of deception. By positioning himself as the only reliable source of information, Trump creates a closed-loop of loyalty and belief among his followers.

Leveraging Cultural References:

Trump's rhetoric often includes cultural references and memes that resonate with his audience. These references create a sense of shared culture and understanding, further solidifying the bond between Trump and his supporters. By tapping into cultural touchstones, Trump makes his message more relatable and impactful. Trump's ability to craft and propagate a compelling narrative of martyrdom has profound implications for American politics and society. His rhetoric not only shapes the perceptions of his supporters but also influences the broader political discourse. By presenting himself as a victim of a rigged system, Trump has managed to maintain a loyal base despite significant legal and political challenges.

However, this narrative comes with significant risks. The persistent undermining of the judiciary and other democratic institutions erodes public trust and can lead to increased polarization and division. As Trump continues to position himself as a political martyr, the potential for civil unrest and further destabilization remains a serious concern.

In this uncharted territory of American politics, the power of narrative cannot be underestimated. Trump's story of victimhood and defiance will likely continue to resonate with many, shaping the political landscape for years to come.

Chapter 4
Legal and Political Fallout

The conviction of former President Donald Trump on 34 felony counts related to hush money payments has sent shockwaves through the political landscape. This chapter delves into the legal ramifications for Trump post-conviction, examines the potential impacts on the Republican Party and the 2024 election, and captures the reactions from key political figures and the public. The interplay between these factors paints a complex picture of the fallout from this unprecedented legal and political event.

Legal Ramifications for Trump Post-Conviction

The conviction of Donald Trump marks a significant moment in American legal history. Being the first former president to be convicted of felonies while still actively pursuing a return to the White House, Trump's legal troubles pose numerous ramifications:

1. Immediate Legal Consequences: Following the conviction, Trump faces potential sentencing which could include fines, restrictions on certain activities, or even incarceration. However, the exact penalties will depend on subsequent court proceedings and appeals.

2. Appeals Process: Trump's legal team is expected to file appeals, challenging the conviction on various grounds. The appeals process could be prolonged, involving multiple courts and potentially reaching the Supreme Court. This ongoing legal battle will likely keep Trump's legal status in the public eye.

3. Financial and Business Impacts: The legal fees associated with the defense and appeal processes will be substantial. Additionally, the conviction could affect Trump's business ventures, with potential loss of business partnerships, licensing deals, and overall brand value. Investors and partners may distance themselves to avoid reputational damage.

4. Eligibility for Public Office: While the U.S. Constitution does not explicitly prevent a convicted felon from running for president, the political and public perception issues surrounding a candidate with such a background could be insurmountable. Legal scholars and political analysts will debate the

implications, but ultimately, the voters' perception will be critical.

Potential Impacts on the Republican Party and the 2024 Election

The fallout from Trump's conviction extends beyond his personal and legal struggles, significantly affecting the Republican Party and the upcoming 2024 election:

1. Party Divisions: The Republican Party is already experiencing internal divisions between Trump loyalists and those seeking to move the party beyond Trump's influence. The conviction exacerbates these tensions, with some members doubling down in their support for Trump, viewing him as a martyr, while others push for new leadership.

2. Primary Dynamics: Trump's legal woes complicate the primary process for the Republican nomination. His base remains steadfast, but mainstream Republicans may rally behind a different candidate, leading to a potentially contentious and fragmented primary season. The outcome of this division could determine the party's strategy and unity heading into the general election.

3. Fundraising and Campaign Strategy: Fundraising efforts for Trump may see both boosts and declines. His core supporters are likely to increase donations in a show of solidarity, while major donors and traditional Republican funders might withdraw support, fearing negative publicity and diminished returns on investment.

4. Electoral Strategy: The 2024 election strategy for the Republican Party will need to address Trump's legal status. Candidates will have to navigate their positions on Trump carefully, balancing appeals to his base with attempts to win over moderate and undecided voters. This delicate balance could influence campaign messaging, policy focuses, and public engagements.

5. Impact on Swing Voters: Swing voters, particularly in key battleground states, will be crucial in the 2024 election. Trump's conviction may sway these voters, with some viewing it as disqualifying, while others may see it as an unjust persecution. The Republican Party's ability to manage this narrative will be pivotal in winning these critical votes.

Reactions from Key Political Figures and the Public

The reactions to Trump's conviction from political figures and the public have been varied and polarized, reflecting the broader divides within American society:

1. Republican Leaders: Key Republican figures have expressed a range of responses. Some, like Senate Minority Leader Mitch McConnell, have been measured in their statements, focusing on the legal process and the presumption of innocence on appeal. Others, like Representatives Marjorie Taylor Greene and Matt Gaetz, have vehemently defended Trump, decrying the conviction as a politically motivated attack.

2. Democratic Leaders: Democrats have largely welcomed the conviction as a sign of accountability and the rule of law. President Joe Biden's remarks have underscored the importance of respecting the judicial process, while other prominent Democrats, like Speaker of the House Nancy Pelosi, have emphasized the need to uphold democratic principles and the integrity of the justice system.

3. Public Opinion: Public reaction has been deeply divided along partisan lines. Polls indicate that a significant portion of Trump's base views the conviction as unjust and politically motivated,

reinforcing their support for him. Conversely, many independents and Democrats see the conviction as a necessary step towards accountability and justice.

4. Media Coverage: Media outlets have played a crucial role in shaping public perception. Conservative media, such as Fox News and Newsmax, have often framed the conviction as part of a broader political witch hunt against Trump. Liberal media, including CNN and MSNBC, have highlighted the legal merits of the case and the importance of accountability. The divergent coverage underscores the polarized media landscape and its influence on public opinion.

5. International Reactions: Globally, Trump's conviction has been met with a mixture of shock, concern, and schadenfreude. Allies and adversaries alike are closely watching the developments, with some viewing it as a test of the resilience of American democracy, while others see it as a confirmation of their criticisms of Trump's leadership.

Analysis of Broader Implications

The broader implications of Trump's conviction and the subsequent fallout are profound, touching on the core aspects of American democracy, the rule of law, and the political landscape:

1. Rule of Law and Accountability: The conviction reinforces the principle that no individual is above the law, even a former president. It serves as a precedent for holding powerful figures accountable for their actions, potentially influencing future legal and political conduct.

2. Democratic Resilience: The handling of Trump's legal case and its fallout will test the resilience of American democratic institutions. Ensuring that the judicial process is perceived as fair and impartial is crucial for maintaining public trust in democracy.

3. Political Polarization: The event has further polarized an already divided nation. The deepening rifts between Trump supporters and opponents highlight the challenges of achieving national unity and consensus on key issues.

4. Future Leadership: The Republican Party's response to Trump's conviction will shape its future leadership and direction. Whether the party continues to embrace Trumpism or moves towards new leadership will have significant implications for American politics.

5. Global Perception: Internationally, the conviction affects how the U.S. is perceived. Allies may see it as a reaffirmation of democratic values, while adversaries may exploit it to criticize American democracy. The global response will impact U.S.

foreign relations and its standing on the world stage. The legal and political fallout from Donald Trump's conviction on 34 felony counts is a landmark event in American history. It highlights the complexities of upholding the rule of law while navigating the intricacies of political dynamics. As the Republican Party grapples with its future direction and the public processes these developments, the broader implications for American democracy are profound. This chapter has explored the immediate legal consequences for Trump, the potential impacts on the Republican Party and the 2024 election, and the varied reactions from political figures and the public. The road ahead is uncertain, but one thing is clear: the fallout from this conviction will reverberate through the American political landscape for years to come.

Chapter 5
The Role of the Judiciary

The judiciary plays a fundamental role in upholding the rule of law and ensuring justice in any democratic society. In the context of Donald Trump's recent convictions, the judicial process has come under intense scrutiny, with significant implications for both the former president and the broader political landscape. This chapter will examine the judicial process in Trump's case, explore the importance of an independent judiciary in a democracy, and provide historical precedents and comparisons to other high-profile cases.

Examination of the Judicial Process in Trump's Case

1. The Indictment and Charges:
Donald Trump faced 34 felony counts related to hush money payments during his 2016 presidential campaign. These charges stemmed from allegations that Trump had orchestrated a scheme to pay off adult film actress Stormy Daniels to prevent her from disclosing an alleged affair. The payments were reportedly made through Trump's former

lawyer, Michael Cohen, who later testified against him. The indictment detailed multiple instances of falsifying business records, a felony under New York law when done to conceal another crime.

2. Pre-Trial Proceedings:

The pre-trial phase involved numerous legal maneuvers from both the prosecution and defense teams. Trump's legal team sought to dismiss the charges on various grounds, arguing that the case was politically motivated and lacked sufficient evidence. The prosecution, led by Manhattan District Attorney Alvin Bragg, countered these motions by emphasizing the robustness of the evidence and the necessity of holding even a former president accountable.

3. The Trial:

The trial took place over five weeks, with the jury being selected through a meticulous process designed to ensure impartiality. The prosecution presented a series of witnesses, including Michael Cohen, who provided testimony on the inner workings of the hush money scheme. Documents and financial records were introduced as evidence to corroborate the claims. The defense aimed to discredit Cohen and other witnesses, portraying them as unreliable and motivated by personal vendettas.

4. The Verdict:
After extensive deliberation, the jury reached a unanimous verdict, convicting Trump on all 34 counts. The decision underscored the principle that no one, regardless of their status or position, is above the law. The verdict was a significant moment in American legal history, marking the first time a former president had been convicted of criminal charges.
5. Post-Trial Reactions:
The aftermath of the verdict saw a flurry of reactions from various quarters. Trump denounced the conviction as a political witch hunt, a claim echoed by many of his supporters. Conversely, proponents of the rule of law hailed the verdict as a testament to the integrity of the judicial system. The case has since been appealed, with Trump's legal team continuing to challenge the conviction.

The Importance of an Independent Judiciary in a Democracy

1. Upholding the Rule of Law:
An independent judiciary is essential for upholding the rule of law, ensuring that all individuals and institutions, including government officials, are subject to the law. The judiciary's independence from political influence is crucial for maintaining

public trust in the legal system and for protecting individual rights and freedoms.

2. Checks and Balances:

In a democratic system, the judiciary serves as a critical check on the powers of the executive and legislative branches. By interpreting and applying the law impartially, the judiciary prevents abuses of power and ensures that government actions comply with constitutional and legal standards. This balance of power is fundamental to the functioning of a healthy democracy.

3. Protecting Civil Liberties:

The judiciary plays a vital role in protecting civil liberties and ensuring that laws and government actions do not infringe upon individual rights. Through judicial review, courts can strike down laws or executive actions that violate constitutional protections, safeguarding the freedoms of speech, assembly, and due process, among others.

4. Maintaining Public Confidence:

Public confidence in the judiciary is essential for the legitimacy of the legal system. An independent judiciary that operates transparently and fairly helps build trust among citizens that justice will be administered impartially. This confidence is particularly important in politically charged cases, where perceptions of bias can undermine the integrity of the judicial process.

5. Historical Context:
The framers of the United States Constitution recognized the importance of an independent judiciary, enshrining this principle in the document's structure. The establishment of a separate judicial branch, with judges appointed for life and insulated from political pressures, reflects the foundational belief that justice must be administered free from external influences.

Historical Precedents and Comparisons to Other High-Profile Cases

1. Watergate Scandal (1972-1974):
The Watergate scandal remains one of the most significant political and legal crises in American history. The break-in at the Democratic National Committee headquarters and the subsequent cover-up led to a series of investigations and legal proceedings that ultimately implicated President Richard Nixon. The role of the judiciary was pivotal in unraveling the scandal, with Judge John Sirica overseeing the trials of the Watergate burglars and the Supreme Court ruling in United States v. Nixon (1974) that Nixon had to release the White House

tapes. This case underscored the judiciary's ability to hold even the highest office accountable.

2. Bill Clinton's Impeachment (1998-1999):

President Bill Clinton's impeachment on charges of perjury and obstruction of justice related to his extramarital affair with Monica Lewinsky was another high-profile case involving the judiciary. The Senate trial highlighted the judiciary's role in interpreting the law and determining the application of constitutional standards in impeachment proceedings. Although Clinton was acquitted by the Senate, the process emphasized the judiciary's function in addressing allegations of misconduct at the highest levels of government.

3. The Trials of the Chicago Seven (1969-1970):

The trial of the Chicago Seven, who were charged with conspiracy and inciting a riot during the 1968 Democratic National Convention, was a landmark case in the context of political dissent and judicial independence. Judge Julius Hoffman's conduct during the trial was widely criticized for perceived bias against the defendants, leading to discussions about the importance of judicial impartiality. The appellate court later overturned the convictions, reinforcing the necessity of fair judicial processes.

4. The O.J. Simpson Trial (1995):

The trial of O.J. Simpson for the murders of Nicole Brown Simpson and Ron Goldman was one of the most publicized and contentious criminal trials in American history. The case highlighted issues of race, media influence, and the functioning of the judicial system. Despite the acquittal, the trial demonstrated the complexities of high-profile cases and the challenges faced by the judiciary in maintaining fairness and impartiality under intense public scrutiny.

5. The Trials of Civil Rights Activists:

Throughout the civil rights movement, numerous activists, including Martin Luther King Jr. and Rosa Parks, faced legal challenges that tested the judiciary's commitment to justice and equality. These trials often brought to light systemic biases within the legal system, prompting judicial and legislative reforms aimed at ensuring equal protection under the law. The judiciary's role in these cases was critical in advancing civil rights and reinforcing the principle of justice for all.

Lessons and Reflections

The judiciary's handling of Donald Trump's case and the subsequent reactions underscore several key lessons about the role of the judiciary in a democracy:

1. Impartiality and Fairness:

The integrity of the judicial process hinges on impartiality and fairness. The selection of an unbiased jury and the adherence to due process are fundamental to ensuring that justice is served without prejudice.

2. Accountability:

The judiciary must hold individuals accountable for their actions, regardless of their status or position. This principle is crucial for maintaining the rule of law and ensuring that no one is above the law.

3. Transparency:

Transparent judicial proceedings help build public trust and confidence in the legal system. Openness in the judicial process allows for public scrutiny and reassures citizens that justice is being administered fairly.

4. Resilience:

The judiciary must remain resilient in the face of political pressures and attempts to undermine its authority. Upholding judicial independence is essential for the continued functioning of a democratic society.

5. Historical Continuity:

Historical precedents demonstrate the enduring importance of an independent judiciary in safeguarding democracy. The lessons learned from past high-profile cases inform current and future judicial practices, ensuring that the judiciary continues to uphold its critical role in society.

The role of the judiciary in the case against Donald Trump highlights the essential function of an independent judicial system in a democracy. By examining the judicial process, understanding the importance of judicial independence, and reflecting on historical precedents, we gain a deeper appreciation for the judiciary's role in upholding the rule of law and ensuring justice. As American democracy navigates uncharted territory, the judiciary stands as a pillar of stability, integrity, and accountability.

Chapter 6
The Media and Public Opinion

Media Coverage of the Trump Convictions and Biden's Comments

The media plays a pivotal role in shaping public perception, especially in politically charged situations. The coverage of former President Donald Trump's 34 felony convictions related to hush money payments and President Joe Biden's subsequent comments has been extensive and varied across different media outlets. This chapter delves into how different segments of the media reported these events and the resulting impact on public opinion.

Media Coverage of Trump's Convictions

From the moment the Manhattan jury delivered its unanimous verdict, the media landscape was flooded with reports, analyses, and opinions. The coverage can broadly be categorized into several types:

1. Mainstream Media: Outlets like CNN, The New York Times, and The Washington Post provided detailed reports on the trial, the evidence presented, and the legal implications of the verdict. These reports focused on the factual aspects of the case, including the charges, the trial process, and the reactions from both legal experts and the public. Additionally, these outlets often highlighted the potential ramifications for Trump's political future.

2. Conservative Media: Fox News, The Wall Street Journal, and Breitbart took a different approach, emphasizing the perspective that the convictions were politically motivated. They often featured segments with Trump's legal team, Republican politicians, and conservative pundits who argued that the case was part of a broader attempt by the Democrats to undermine Trump. This narrative resonated strongly with Trump's base, reinforcing the idea of a biased justice system.

3. Progressive Media: Outlets such as MSNBC, The Guardian, and HuffPost generally portrayed the verdict as a triumph of justice and accountability. Their coverage frequently included interviews with legal analysts who supported the legitimacy of the trial and emphasized the importance of upholding the rule of law.

4. International Media: Global outlets like BBC, Al Jazeera, and The Economist provided an international perspective on the events. These reports often compared the American legal and political systems with those of other countries, offering a broader context and analyzing the potential global implications of Trump's legal troubles.

Biden's Comments and Media Reactions

President Joe Biden's comments on Trump's convictions were equally scrutinized. Biden's statements were designed to reinforce confidence in the American judicial system and to highlight the dangers of undermining it for political gain.

1. Supportive Coverage: Many mainstream and progressive media outlets echoed Biden's sentiments, emphasizing the importance of respecting judicial processes. They often cited Biden's assertion that questioning the legitimacy of the justice system was "reckless, dangerous, and downright irresponsible."

2. Critical Coverage: Conservative media criticized Biden for his remarks, accusing him of using the situation to distract from his administration's challenges and the legal issues facing his son,

Hunter Biden. They also argued that Biden's comments were politically motivated, aiming to weaken Trump's standing ahead of the 2024 election.

3. Neutral Coverage: Some media outlets maintained a more neutral stance, simply reporting Biden's comments without much editorializing. They focused on providing a balanced view, presenting both Biden's perspective and the criticisms leveled against him.

Analysis of Public Opinion Polls and Their Implications

Public opinion polls provide valuable insights into how these events and their coverage have influenced the electorate. Several reputable polling organizations conducted surveys to gauge public sentiment in the aftermath of Trump's convictions and Biden's comments.

General Public Sentiment

1. Trust in the Judicial System: Polls indicated a stark divide in public trust in the judicial system, largely along partisan lines. A majority of Democrats expressed confidence in the fairness of Trump's trial and the judicial process, while a significant portion of Republicans viewed the trial as politically motivated.

2. Impact on Trump's Support Base: Despite the convictions, Trump maintained strong support among his base. Polls showed that a substantial percentage of his supporters believed the charges were part of a larger political conspiracy against him. This unwavering support suggests that Trump's narrative of victimization continues to resonate deeply with his core voters.

3. Biden's Approval Ratings: Biden's approval ratings saw a slight increase following his comments on the importance of upholding the judicial system. This suggests that his message of protecting democratic institutions may have had a positive impact, particularly among independents and moderate voters.

Specific Poll Findings

1. ABC News/Washington Post Poll: This poll found that 56% of Americans believed Trump's trial was conducted fairly, while 38% thought it was politically motivated. Among Republicans, however, 65% viewed the trial as unfair, illustrating the deep partisan divide.

2. Pew Research Center Poll: According to this poll, 60% of Democrats felt more confident in the judicial system after the verdict, compared to only 20% of Republicans. The poll also indicated that Biden's comments were well-received among Democrats and independents, with 70% of

Democrats and 55% of independents agreeing that it was important to respect the verdict.

3. Gallup Poll: This survey showed a small uptick in Biden's overall approval rating, rising from 43% to 46% following his comments. The increase was particularly notable among younger voters and those with higher education levels, suggesting that Biden's emphasis on democratic principles resonated with these groups.

Implications of Poll Results

1. Election Strategies: The poll results suggest that both Trump and Biden will likely continue to leverage these narratives in their campaign strategies. Trump is expected to double down on his claims of a rigged system to galvanize his base, while Biden will likely emphasize the importance of judicial integrity and democratic norms to appeal to a broader electorate.

2. Voter Mobilization: The deep partisan divide highlighted by the polls underscores the challenge both candidates face in mobilizing voters. For Trump, the key will be maintaining the loyalty of his base, while Biden will need to focus on convincing independents and moderate Republicans that his administration is committed to upholding democratic values.

3. Media's Role: The media's role in shaping public opinion is evident from the poll results. Different narratives presented by various media outlets have significantly influenced how their respective audiences perceive the events. This reinforces the importance of media literacy and the need for consumers to critically evaluate the information they receive.

The Influence of Media Narratives on the Political Landscape

The media does not just report on events; it helps shape the political narrative and, by extension, the political landscape. The coverage of Trump's convictions and Biden's comments has highlighted several key aspects of this influence.

Media Bias and Partisan Divides

1. Selective Reporting: Media outlets often choose which aspects of a story to emphasize based on their target audience. For example, conservative media focused heavily on potential political motivations behind Trump's convictions, while progressive media emphasized the integrity of the judicial process. This selective reporting can reinforce existing biases and deepen partisan divides.

2. Framing and Language: The language used in media reports also plays a crucial role. Terms like "unprecedented," "politically motivated," and "judicial integrity" carry different connotations and can influence how readers perceive the events. The framing of Biden's comments as either a defense of democracy or a political maneuver significantly impacts public perception.

3. Echo Chambers: The proliferation of echo chambers, where individuals consume media that reinforces their preexisting beliefs, further polarize public opinion. This phenomenon was evident in the differing responses to the Trump verdict and Biden's comments, with audiences largely aligning with the perspectives presented by their preferred media outlets.

Impact on Political Campaigns

1. Narrative Control: Both Trump and Biden have sought to control the narrative through their interactions with the media. Trump's claims of a rigged system and Biden's emphasis on judicial integrity are strategic moves aimed at shaping public opinion and mobilizing their respective bases.

2. Media Endorsements and Criticism: Endorsements from media personalities and criticism from opposing outlets can significantly impact a candidate's image. Positive coverage can

bolster a candidate's standing, while negative reports can damage their reputation and credibility.

3. Campaign Messaging: The themes emphasized by media coverage influence campaign messaging. For instance, Trump's campaign has capitalized on conservative media's portrayal of the verdict as unjust, using it to rally his supporters. Conversely, Biden's campaign has highlighted the positive reception of his comments on the judicial system to appeal to undecided voters and reinforce his commitment to democratic principles.

Long-Term Implications

1. Public Trust in Institutions: The media's portrayal of these events has broader implications for public trust in institutions. Consistent narratives about a "rigged" system can erode trust in the judiciary, while positive coverage of judicial processes can reinforce confidence in the rule of law.

2. Democratic Resilience: The way media outlets cover challenges to democratic norms, such as the January 6th Capitol riot and Trump's refusal to accept the 2020 election results, plays a crucial role in shaping public understanding of democratic resilience. Balanced and factual reporting can help foster a more informed and engaged electorate.

3. Future Political Contests: The influence of media narratives on current events will likely extend to

future political contests. The themes of judicial integrity, political accountability, and media bias will continue to shape voter perceptions and campaign strategies.

The media's coverage of Trump's convictions and Biden's comments has profoundly influenced public opinion and the political landscape. Through selective reporting, framing, and the creation of echo chambers, the media has played a crucial role in shaping the narratives that define this moment in American politics. Public opinion polls reveal a deeply divided electorate, with trust in the judicial system and political figures varying significantly along partisan lines. As both Trump and Biden prepare for the upcoming election, their ability to control the narrative and leverage media coverage will be pivotal in determining their success. Ultimately, the media's role in shaping public perception underscores the importance of media literacy and the need for

Chapter 7
Hunter Biden's Case

Overview of the Federal Gun Case Against Hunter Biden

Hunter Biden, the son of President Joe Biden, has been a subject of intense media scrutiny and political controversy, particularly surrounding his federal gun case. The case centers on allegations that Hunter Biden made false statements on a federal firearms application. In October 2018, Hunter Biden purchased a firearm, and on the application, he allegedly denied using or being addicted to controlled substances. This denial is significant because, at the time, Hunter Biden was struggling with addiction, which he has openly acknowledged in his memoir and public statements. The case against Hunter Biden is not just about his personal struggles but also about the legal implications of providing false information on a federal firearms application. According to federal law, it is illegal for a person to falsely state their non-use of illegal drugs when purchasing a firearm. This law aims to prevent individuals who may pose a risk, due to substance abuse or other factors, from obtaining firearms.

Hunter Biden's legal troubles began to surface more prominently during his father's presidential campaign, attracting significant media attention and political debate. The case took a more definitive turn when it was reported that the U.S. Attorney's Office in Delaware was investigating Hunter Biden's financial and business activities, including his gun purchase. The investigation was part of a broader inquiry into Hunter Biden's finances, including his taxes and international business dealings.

In June 2021, Hunter Biden reached a tentative agreement with federal prosecutors to resolve the gun charge and tax-related issues. The agreement included a plan for Hunter Biden to plead guilty to two misdemeanor tax charges and enter into a pretrial diversion agreement regarding the gun charge. Pretrial diversion is an alternative to prosecution that allows defendants to avoid a conviction by fulfilling certain requirements, such as undergoing treatment or community service. In this case, it was reported that Hunter Biden would avoid prosecution on the gun charge if he completed a program addressing his drug addiction.

Media and Political Reactions to Hunter Biden's Legal Issues

The media and political reactions to Hunter Biden's legal troubles have been intense and polarized. Media coverage has varied significantly across different outlets, with some focusing on the legal aspects and Hunter Biden's personal struggles, while others have framed the issue as indicative of broader political corruption.

Mainstream media outlets like CNN, The New York Times, and The Washington Post have reported extensively on the legal proceedings, Hunter Biden's addiction struggles, and the implications for President Joe Biden's administration. These outlets often highlight the personal aspect of the story, noting Hunter Biden's public acknowledgment of his addiction and his efforts to seek treatment. They also emphasize the legal process, explaining the nature of the charges and the potential outcomes.

In contrast, conservative media outlets such as Fox News, The Wall Street Journal, and The New York Post have framed the story in a more politically charged context. These outlets often suggest that Hunter Biden's legal troubles reflect poorly on his father's administration and imply potential corruption or favoritism in how the case is being handled. Fox News, for example, has frequently featured segments questioning the integrity of the investigation and suggesting that Hunter Biden is receiving preferential treatment because of his father's position. The political reactions have been equally divided. Republicans have seized upon Hunter Biden's legal issues as a key point of criticism against President Joe Biden. Prominent Republican figures, including former President Donald Trump, have used the case to suggest that the Biden family is corrupt and that the President is involved in improper or illegal activities. Trump and his supporters often reference Hunter Biden's business dealings in Ukraine and China, framing the gun case as part of a broader narrative of alleged misconduct. During rallies and interviews, Trump has repeatedly brought up Hunter Biden's case, arguing that it exemplifies a double standard in the justice system. Trump and his allies claim that if any member of his family were facing similar charges, the media and the legal system would treat them more harshly. This narrative is designed to resonate with Trump's base, many of whom believe that the mainstream media and the legal system are biased against conservatives. Democrats, on the other hand, have largely defended Hunter Biden and President Joe Biden. They emphasize Hunter Biden's struggles with addiction as a personal issue and stress the importance of treating addiction as a health issue rather than a criminal one. Democratic supporters argue that Hunter Biden is taking responsibility for his actions and undergoing the appropriate legal process. They also point out that the investigation into Hunter Biden began under the Trump administration, suggesting that it is being handled in a non-partisan manner.

President Biden has addressed the issue by expressing support for his son and confidence in the legal process. He has stated that he believes in his son's honesty and integrity and that Hunter Biden will continue to work through his challenges. This stance is intended to show a compassionate and supportive family dynamic while also reinforcing the idea that the legal system should be allowed to operate independently.

How This Case Is Used by Trump and His Supporters to Counter Biden's Criticisms

The case against Hunter Biden has become a key talking point for Trump and his supporters as they seek to counter criticisms from President Biden and the Democratic Party. Trump has consistently used the legal troubles of Hunter Biden to deflect attention from his own legal issues and to paint the Biden administration as corrupt and hypocritical.

One of the main strategies employed by Trump and his allies is to highlight what they perceive as a double standard in the treatment of political figures and their families. Trump argues that the media and the legal system are lenient with Hunter Biden while being excessively harsh on him and his associates. This argument is designed to undermine the credibility of the investigations and legal proceedings against Trump, suggesting that they are politically motivated.

In speeches and social media posts, Trump frequently references Hunter Biden's case to question the integrity of the justice system. He claims that if the son of a Republican president were facing similar charges, the response from the media and the legal system would be much more severe. By making this comparison, Trump aims to rally his supporters around the idea that he is being unfairly targeted and that his legal troubles are part of a broader effort to undermine his political career. Trump's campaign has also used Hunter Biden's case as a focal point in their attacks on President Biden's credibility and fitness for office. They argue that President Biden's inability to control or influence his son's behavior reflects poorly on his leadership and decision-making abilities. This line of attack is intended to cast doubt on President

Biden's moral authority and to suggest that he is incapable of maintaining ethical standards within his own family, let alone the country.

Furthermore, Trump and his supporters have leveraged Hunter Biden's case to distract from Trump's own legal challenges. Whenever new developments arise in Trump's legal battles, his campaign often responds by bringing up Hunter Biden's case, aiming to shift the narrative and focus public attention on the Biden family's issues. This tactic is intended to create a sense of equivalence between the two situations, suggesting that both families are embroiled in controversy and legal troubles. The conservative media has played a significant role in amplifying this narrative. Outlets like Fox News and The New York Post frequently cover Hunter Biden's case, providing a steady stream of content that reinforces Trump's talking points. These media outlets often present the story in a way that emphasizes potential corruption and misconduct, keeping the issue in the public eye and maintaining its relevance as a political tool.

In addition to media coverage, social media platforms have been a battleground for narratives surrounding Hunter Biden's case. Trump's supporters actively share and discuss news related to Hunter Biden, using hashtags and trending topics to keep the issue prominent. This online activity helps to sustain the narrative and ensures that it remains a point of contention in political discussions. Overall, the case against Hunter Biden has become a central element in the political strategy of Trump and his supporters. By framing the issue as indicative of broader corruption and a double standard in the justice system, they aim to undermine President Biden's credibility, distract from Trump's own legal challenges, and rally their base around a shared sense of grievance and injustice. This approach highlights the deeply polarized nature of contemporary American politics, where legal issues are not just matters of law but also potent political weapons.

Chapter 8
The Election Dynamics

As the 2024 presidential election approaches, the legal battles faced by both President Joe Biden and former President Donald Trump have become pivotal elements shaping the campaign landscape. These legal issues not only influence public perception but also dictate the strategies and messaging of both campaigns. This chapter delves into how these legal battles are affecting the election dynamics, the strategies employed by Biden and Trump to navigate these challenges, and the potential scenarios and outcomes that could arise.

Legal Battles Shaping the Election

Trump's Legal Troubles

Former President Donald Trump's legal issues, particularly his conviction on 34 felony counts related to hush money payments, have cast a long shadow over his campaign. This case, which centers on payments made during his 2016 campaign to silence allegations of an extramarital affair, has led to a significant legal and political predicament for Trump. The conviction has provided ammunition for his critics and a rallying point for his supporters, who view the prosecution as a politically motivated attack. Trump's narrative that the justice system is "rigged" against him has resonated with a segment of his base, fueling a sense of grievance and mistrust towards the judiciary. This sentiment has become a cornerstone of his campaign, with Trump positioning himself as a martyr of a corrupt system. However, this strategy also carries risks, as it alienates moderate voters and reinforces the perception of Trump as a divisive figure.

Biden's Response to Trump's Conviction

President Joe Biden has seized upon Trump's legal woes to draw a sharp contrast between himself and his predecessor. In speeches and public statements, Biden has emphasized the integrity of the justice system and the importance of respecting judicial outcomes. By framing Trump's attacks on the judiciary as reckless and dangerous, Biden aims to present himself as a defender of democratic institutions and the rule of law.

This strategy not only bolsters Biden's image as a steady and principled leader but also seeks to undermine Trump's credibility. Biden's insistence that the justice system is not rigged and that Trump's conviction was a fair and just outcome serves to reinforce his campaign's message of stability and integrity. However, Biden must also navigate his own set of legal challenges, particularly the federal gun case involving his son, Hunter Biden.

Hunter Biden's Legal Issues

The federal gun case against Hunter Biden has been a source of contention and a focal point for Trump's attacks on President Biden. The case, which involves allegations of false statements on a firearm purchase form, has been used by Trump and his supporters to suggest hypocrisy and corruption within the Biden family. Trump's campaign has repeatedly highlighted Hunter Biden's legal troubles, attempting to draw a parallel between the accusations against Hunter and the convictions against Trump.

President Biden's approach to his son's legal issues has been to maintain a degree of separation, emphasizing the independence of the judiciary and the need for due process. By avoiding direct involvement, Biden aims to uphold the principle that no one is above the law, including his own family. However, this stance also exposes him to criticism and scrutiny, particularly from those who view the case as a reflection of broader ethical concerns.

Campaign Strategies

Trump's Campaign Strategy

Trump's strategy in light of his legal battles has been multifaceted, focusing on rallying his base, deflecting attention from his convictions, and attacking Biden's credibility. Central to this strategy is the narrative of victimization and persecution, which Trump uses to galvanize his supporters and frame himself as a champion of the "forgotten" Americans who feel disenfranchised by the political system.

1. Rallying the Base: Trump's core supporters are deeply loyal, and his portrayal of the legal system as biased against him has strengthened their resolve. Trump's campaign events and rallies emphasize themes of injustice and resilience, seeking to create a sense of solidarity and defiance among his followers.

2. Deflection and Distraction: Trump's team has employed tactics to shift the focus away from his legal troubles and towards broader political and social issues. By highlighting economic concerns, immigration, and foreign policy, Trump aims to redirect public discourse and diminish the impact of his convictions on his campaign.

3. Attacking Biden: Trump has not shied away from attacking Biden on multiple fronts, particularly regarding Hunter Biden's legal issues. By framing the case as emblematic of corruption and nepotism, Trump seeks to undermine Biden's moral authority and question his integrity.

Biden's Campaign Strategy

In contrast, Biden's campaign strategy revolves around promoting stability, integrity, and competence. Biden aims to present himself as a stark contrast to Trump, emphasizing his commitment to democratic principles and effective governance.

1. Highlighting Stability: Biden's messaging focuses on his administration's achievements and the importance of continuity in leadership. By showcasing policy successes and progress on key issues such as the economy, healthcare, and climate change, Biden seeks to reassure voters of his steady hand in turbulent times.

2. Defending Democracy: Biden has positioned himself as a defender of democratic institutions, repeatedly stressing the importance of respecting judicial outcomes and electoral processes. This emphasis on the rule of law and the integrity of the justice system aims to counter Trump's narrative of a "rigged" system.

3. Addressing Legal Challenges: While Biden has largely avoided direct commentary on Hunter Biden's case, his campaign has emphasized the need for transparency and accountability. By maintaining a principled stance and allowing the legal process to unfold without interference, Biden aims to uphold his image as a leader committed to justice and fairness.

Potential Scenarios and Outcomes

Scenario 1: Trump's Legal Troubles Deepen
If Trump faces additional legal challenges or new convictions, the impact on his campaign could be significant. While his core supporters may remain loyal, further legal setbacks could erode support among moderate and undecided voters. In this scenario, Biden could capitalize on the heightened perception of Trump as a liability, reinforcing his own image as a stable and trustworthy leader.

Scenario 2: Hunter Biden's Case Escalates
Should Hunter Biden's legal issues escalate, it could pose a considerable challenge for President Biden's campaign. Increased media scrutiny and political attacks from Trump could force Biden to address the issue more directly, potentially diverting attention from his policy achievements and campaign messaging. This scenario could narrow the perceived gap in integrity between the two

candidates, complicating Biden's efforts to position himself as a moral contrast to Trump.

Scenario 3: Legal Battles Become Central to the Election

If legal battles dominate the election discourse, both campaigns may find themselves focusing more on defending their respective positions than on substantive policy debates. This could lead to a highly polarized and contentious election environment, with voters being swayed more by perceptions of integrity and justice than by policy platforms. In this scenario, the candidate who can most effectively navigate and mitigate the impact of their legal challenges may gain a crucial advantage.

Scenario 4: Public Fatigue and Shift to Policy Issues

Alternatively, public fatigue with the constant focus on legal battles could lead to a shift in voter priorities towards policy issues. If voters become weary of the legal drama, both campaigns may need to pivot back to discussing their visions for the future. In this case, the candidate with the most compelling and forward-looking policy proposals could gain momentum.

The legal battles of both Trump and Biden are undeniably shaping the dynamics of the 2024 election. As each candidate navigates their respective challenges, their strategies and the public's perception of their integrity and leadership will play a critical role in determining the outcome. Whether the focus remains on legal issues or shifts to policy debates, the election promises to be a defining moment for American democracy, with profound implications for the future direction of the country.

Chapter 9
The Future of American Democracy

The political landscape in the United States has been dramatically altered by the events surrounding the Biden-Trump showdown. As we explore the broader implications of this confrontation for American democracy, it is essential to understand how these dynamics challenge the resilience of democratic institutions in times of political crisis. This chapter will delve into the lessons learned from this tumultuous period and chart a path forward for preserving and strengthening democracy in America.

The Broader Implications of the Biden-Trump Showdown

The intense political battle between President Joe Biden and former President Donald Trump has far-reaching consequences for the American democratic system. At the core of this confrontation are issues of trust in democratic institutions, the rule of law, and the integrity of the electoral process.

1. Trust in Democratic Institutions

One of the most significant implications of the Biden-Trump showdown is the erosion of trust in democratic institutions. Trump's repeated claims of a "rigged" justice system and "stolen" elections have resonated with a substantial portion of the American electorate. This rhetoric has sown doubt about the fairness and legitimacy of the judicial and electoral processes.

- Judiciary: Trump's conviction on 34 felony counts related to hush money payments has been framed by his supporters as a politically motivated attack. Despite the trial being conducted according to standard judicial procedures, the narrative of a biased system has gained traction, undermining confidence in the judiciary's impartiality.

- Electoral System: The aftermath of the 2020 presidential election saw unprecedented challenges to the electoral process, culminating in the January 6th Capitol riot. Trump's refusal to accept the election results and subsequent claims of widespread fraud have led to increased polarization and skepticism about the integrity of future elections.

2. The Rule of Law

The principle that no one is above the law is fundamental to American democracy. Trump's legal troubles have tested this principle, highlighting both strengths and vulnerabilities in the justice system.

- Accountability: The conviction of a former president demonstrates that the legal system can hold even the highest officeholders accountable for their actions. This is a crucial affirmation of the rule of law.

- Perception of Bias: However, the perception of political bias in the legal proceedings against Trump has fueled divisions. Ensuring that the justice system is seen as fair and impartial is vital for maintaining public trust.

3. Political Polarization

The Biden-Trump showdown has exacerbated political polarization in the United States. The sharp divide between supporters of the two leaders reflects deeper societal fractures.

- Media and Communication: Media coverage and social media have amplified partisan narratives, making it challenging to find common ground. Echo chambers and misinformation contribute to a polarized environment where constructive dialogue is increasingly rare.

- Identity Politics: The conflict between Biden and Trump is often framed in terms of identity politics, with each side viewing the other as an existential threat. This polarization hampers efforts to address critical issues through bipartisan cooperation.

Resilience of Democratic Institutions in Times of Political Crisis

Despite the significant challenges posed by the Biden-Trump showdown, American democratic institutions have shown remarkable resilience. Understanding how these institutions have weathered the storm can provide valuable insights into safeguarding democracy in the future.

1. The Judiciary

The judicial system has played a crucial role in upholding the rule of law during this period of political turmoil.

- Fair Trials: The conviction of Trump involved a meticulous legal process, demonstrating the judiciary's ability to conduct fair trials even under intense public scrutiny.

- Judicial Independence: Judges and legal professionals have largely maintained their independence, resisting pressures to politicize their decisions. This independence is vital for ensuring that justice is administered impartially.

2. The Electoral System

The resilience of the electoral system has been tested but ultimately upheld during recent elections.

- Election Security: Despite baseless claims of widespread fraud, multiple audits and recounts have confirmed the integrity of the electoral process. This underscores the robustness of the mechanisms in place to ensure fair elections.
- Peaceful Transfer of Power: The peaceful transfer of power, a cornerstone of democratic stability, was maintained despite the January 6th insurrection. This demonstrates the strength of democratic norms and institutions in times of crisis.

3. Media and Civil Society

A free press and active civil society are essential components of a resilient democracy.

- Investigative Journalism: The media has played a critical role in uncovering facts and holding leaders accountable. Investigative journalism has been instrumental in providing the public with accurate information about the actions of political figures.
- Activism and Advocacy: Civil society organizations and activists have mobilized to defend democratic principles, promote voter engagement, and advocate for reforms. This civic engagement is crucial for maintaining a vibrant democracy.

Lessons Learned and the Path Forward

The Biden-Trump showdown offers several key lessons for the future of American democracy. By learning from these experiences, we can take steps to strengthen democratic institutions and foster a more inclusive political environment.

1. Strengthening Electoral Integrity

Ensuring the integrity of elections is paramount for restoring trust in the democratic process.

- Election Reforms: Implementing reforms to enhance transparency, security, and accessibility in the electoral system can help build public confidence. Measures such as modernizing voting infrastructure, ensuring accurate voter rolls, and expanding access to voting can strengthen the process.

- Combating Misinformation: Addressing misinformation and disinformation is critical for protecting electoral integrity. Efforts to promote media literacy and fact-checking can help voters make informed decisions.

2. Upholding the Rule of Law

Maintaining the rule of law requires a commitment to fairness, accountability, and impartiality in the justice system.

- Judicial Reforms: Reforms to ensure the independence and impartiality of the judiciary are essential. This includes measures to protect judges from political pressure and enhance transparency in judicial appointments.

- Accountability Mechanisms: Strengthening mechanisms for accountability, including oversight bodies and ethical standards, can help prevent abuses of power and ensure that all individuals are subject to the law.

3. Reducing Political Polarization

Addressing political polarization is crucial for fostering a more cooperative and productive political environment.

- Promoting Dialogue: Encouraging dialogue and understanding between different political and social groups can help bridge divides. Initiatives that facilitate conversations across partisan lines can reduce hostility and build common ground.

- Civic Education: Investing in civic education can equip citizens with the knowledge and skills needed to engage constructively in the democratic process. This includes understanding the importance of democratic principles, institutions, and norms.

4. Empowering Civil Society

A robust civil society is vital for defending democracy and promoting active citizenship.

- Supporting Activism: Providing support for grassroots organizations and activists working to advance democratic values can strengthen civil society. This includes funding, training, and resources to enhance their impact.

- Encouraging Participation: Encouraging broader participation in civic and political activities can help ensure that diverse voices are represented in the democratic process. This includes efforts to engage underrepresented communities and promote inclusive practices.

5. Ensuring Media Freedom

A free and independent press is essential for holding power to account and informing the public.

- Protecting Journalists: Safeguarding the rights and safety of journalists is crucial for media freedom. This includes legal protections and measures to prevent harassment and violence against journalists.

- Promoting Quality Journalism: Supporting quality journalism through funding, training, and ethical standards can enhance the role of the media in democracy. This includes initiatives to combat misinformation and promote accurate reporting.

The Biden-Trump showdown has underscored the importance of resilience in American democratic institutions. While the challenges are significant, the lessons learned from this period can guide efforts to strengthen democracy and ensure its continued vitality. By committing to electoral integrity, upholding the rule of law, reducing polarization, empowering civil society, and ensuring media freedom, we can build a more robust and inclusive democratic system for future generations. The path forward requires vigilance, cooperation, and a steadfast commitment to the principles that underpin American democracy.

Conclusion
Reflecting on a Tumultuous Era

The political landscape of the United States has been reshaped by unprecedented events, and understanding these changes is crucial for appreciating the current state of American democracy. In this conclusion, we will reflect on the key points discussed throughout this book, delve into the significance of this period in American political history, and issue a call to action for readers to stay informed and engaged in the democratic process.

Summary of the Key Points Discussed in the Book

1. Trump's Convictions:

   - Former President Donald Trump was convicted on 34 felony counts related to hush money payments during his 2016 presidential campaign. This legal battle, covered in detail, revealed the complexities of the American judicial system and its intersection with high-stakes politics.

- The convictions underscored the importance of accountability and the rule of law, even for those who hold or have held the highest office in the land.

2. Biden's Response:

- President Joe Biden's remarks at a fundraiser in Greenwich, Connecticut, highlighted his concerns about Trump's reaction to the convictions. Biden emphasized the danger of undermining the judiciary and democracy by labeling the legal process as "rigged."

- Biden's response framed the election as a critical juncture for the preservation of democratic norms and institutions.

3. Trump's Narrative and Strategy:

- Trump's claims of a rigged system and his portrayal of himself as a political martyr resonated with his base, raising questions about the influence of rhetoric on public perception.

- The former president's strategy to leverage his legal troubles as a rallying cry for his supporters illustrated the deepening polarization in American politics.

4. Impact on the Republican Party:

- The convictions and subsequent fallout had significant implications for the Republican Party, revealing fractures and divergent strategies within the party.

- The party's response to Trump's legal issues and its alignment with or against him became a defining factor in the lead-up to the 2024 election.

5. The Role of the Judiciary:

- The book explored the critical role of the judiciary in upholding the rule of law and maintaining public trust in the justice system.

- The challenges faced by the judiciary in navigating politically charged cases were highlighted, demonstrating the importance of an independent and impartial judicial system.

6. Media and Public Opinion:

- Media coverage played a crucial role in shaping public opinion on Trump's convictions and Biden's response. The book examined how different media outlets presented the events and the resulting impact on public perception.

- Public opinion polls and analyses provided insights into the shifting political landscape and voter sentiments.

7. Hunter Biden's Case:

- The federal gun case against Hunter Biden was discussed as a parallel narrative, illustrating the complexities of personal legal issues intersecting with political dynamics.

- The case was used by Trump and his supporters to counter Biden's criticisms, highlighting the political weaponization of personal legal troubles.

8. Election Dynamics:

   - The 2024 election emerged as a high-stakes contest, with both legal battles and political strategies influencing the campaigns.

   - The potential scenarios and outcomes were explored, emphasizing the critical importance of voter engagement and participation in the democratic process.

9. Future of American Democracy:

   - The broader implications of the Biden-Trump showdown for American democracy were discussed, highlighting the resilience of democratic institutions amidst political crises.

   - The book concluded with lessons learned from this tumultuous era and the path forward for ensuring the health and vitality of American democracy.

Final Thoughts on the Significance of This Period in American Political History

The period covered in this book represents one of the most significant and tumultuous eras in American political history. The convergence of legal battles, political rhetoric, and deep-seated polarization has tested the foundations of the

American democratic system in unprecedented ways.

1. Legal Precedents and Accountability:

- The convictions of a former president on felony charges set a historic precedent, reinforcing the principle that no one is above the law. This period will be remembered for its affirmation of accountability, regardless of political power or influence.

2. Democratic Resilience:

- Despite the challenges posed by political rhetoric and attempts to undermine the judiciary, the resilience of democratic institutions has been a defining feature of this era. The ability of the judicial system to operate independently and deliver verdicts based on evidence underscores the strength of American democracy.

3. Polarization and Public Discourse:

- The deepening polarization and the role of public discourse in shaping political outcomes have been starkly evident. The divergent narratives and strategies employed by political figures have highlighted the need for critical thinking and media literacy among the electorate.

4. The Role of Leadership:

- Leadership during this period has played a pivotal role in guiding the nation through crises. The contrasting approaches of Biden and Trump have provided a study in leadership styles, with significant implications for the future of American governance.

5. Engagement and Participation:
   - The events of this period have underscored the importance of civic engagement and participation in the democratic process. The active involvement of citizens in voting, advocacy, and informed discourse is crucial for the health of democracy.

Call to Action for Readers

As we reflect on this tumultuous era, it is imperative to recognize the role each of us plays in shaping the future of American democracy. The following call to action aims to inspire readers to stay informed, engaged, and proactive in their civic duties:

1. Stay Informed:
   - Knowledge is power. Stay informed about current events, legal developments, and political dynamics. Seek out reputable news sources and critically evaluate information to form well-rounded perspectives.

2. Engage in Civil Discourse:
   - Engage in respectful and informed discussions with others. Civil discourse is essential for bridging divides and fostering mutual understanding. Listen

to diverse viewpoints and contribute thoughtfully to conversations.

3. Participate in the Democratic Process:

- Exercise your right to vote in every election, from local to national. Your vote is a powerful tool for shaping the direction of your community and country. Encourage others to participate and make their voices heard.

4. Support Democratic Institutions:

- Advocate for the integrity and independence of democratic institutions, including the judiciary and the electoral system. Support efforts to uphold the rule of law and protect the principles of democracy.

5. Promote Accountability:

- Hold leaders accountable for their actions and decisions. Advocate for transparency, ethical governance, and adherence to the rule of law. Support candidates and initiatives that prioritize accountability and integrity.

6. Foster Media Literacy:

- Develop and promote media literacy skills to navigate the complex information landscape. Learn to discern credible sources from misinformation and contribute to a well-informed public discourse.

7. Advocate for Reforms:

- Support reforms that strengthen democratic processes and institutions. Advocate for policies that promote transparency, reduce corruption, and enhance public trust in governance.

8. Build Community and Solidarity:

- Foster a sense of community and solidarity with others. Work together to address common challenges and support initiatives that promote social cohesion and collective well-being.

Final Reflection

The period we have examined in this book has been marked by significant challenges and profound changes. Yet, it has also demonstrated the enduring strength and resilience of American democracy. As we move forward, let us carry with us the lessons learned and the commitment to uphold the values that define our democratic society.

By staying informed, engaged, and proactive, we can contribute to a brighter future for our nation. Together, we can navigate the complexities of our time and ensure that the principles of democracy continue to thrive.

Thank you for taking this journey through one of the most consequential periods in American political history. May this book serve as a reminder of the power of informed and engaged citizenship and the enduring importance of democracy in our lives.